Life Is A Journey

Live ,Dream ,Believe,Achieve 

Sarita Gupta

BookLeaf Publishing

India | USA | UK

Dedication

My mom......Heart full of love, always smiling and lips
always showering blessings
Spreading cheer and happiness.
Always ready to accommodate others needs, lovingly
helping all
An ideal daughter, wife, sister, mother, grandmother and
a guide for all
I always wondered how were these many titles never a
bother
Was she a human or an angel, such an excellent example
to follow
So many miss her presence, to describe her loss, words
are not ample⌧⌧

Preface

These small poems are almost every Woman's life story and exams through the years.
Every woman who puts family ahead of herself trying to balance but mostly fail in others eyes - Stop and get up again to fulfil your dreams

From being an independent, strong headed person transforming to an emotionally dependent person, family keeping away from their focus

Mostly the children bring them back from slumber of self doubt to make tough decisions, taking baby steps again towards new challenging but exciting journey

For all who hesitate in taking that 1st step ...
For all who think Woman can never be another Woman's best friend..
For all the people who let other's decide for them..
For all the dreamers, life is not about the age but about how and when we decide to break our mental cage..

Acknowledgements

To all who made me who I am today....

My Ma Smt. Vijay Lakshmi Negi (because of her the thoughts became words)and Papa Shri Darmiyan Singh Negi 🖤 🖤 🖤
For fighting to keep me alive when all doctors said I cannot survive...
Mom Kamla Gupta 🖤 🖤 🖤 for all the love, blessings and strength which she showers upon me always.....

Grateful and blessed for their love and support for every decision I make in life, till today..

Heartfelt Gratitude to my Big Family who have been my cheerleaders throughout

My children Tanay and Chahel for always believing in our visions and dreams ⊠⊠ especially transforming me back to be what i was in my young age, strong, risktaker, believer and achiever 🖤 🖤 🖤

1. Real Life Heroes

Who needed heroes when we were lucky to have Ma
and Pa always?
They pushed their needs back so we could pave our
lives our ways.
They let our hearts bloom slowly to allow our
imaginations touch the sky,
We were their little birds who, with their support, were
never afraid to fly.
They made us independent but also taught us about
values and responsibility,
We were ready to take risks in new fields and never
doubted our capability.
They always taught us to be prepared to fight and never
bother about the result,
Their small teachings and guidance have shaped us today
as adults,
Our heroes couldn't fly or didn't carry a magic wand, But
their simple love turned our dreams into a lifelong bond.
Through storms and trials, they stood in front of us
unwavering,

While in their shadow, we learned that kindness is also brave and daring.
Wherever we are in the world, what holds us together is our love bond,
A tapestry of memories that time can't quite abscond. In laughter and tears, in whispers and song,
Ma and Pa's love are the roots where we all belong💕 💕

2. Learning's of Life

Learning's of life can tear us apart and leave a bitter
sweet taste
At times it fills heart with happiness and at times life
seems a waste

Happiness depends on the time and effort we put in our
relations
But we waste our energy in calculating our returns and
expectations

It is true that our feelings should be reciprocated for sure
Otherwise someone's casual and cold approach makes us
unsure

Friends fill up the void which we feel so heavily
We put on a big smile and can face problems easily

Small things, small chats, some fun, some laughter that
we share
Reciprocating to all our relations with respect and love

shows that we care

In moments of darkness, when shadows stretch long,
It's in love's gentle whispers where we find our song.

Lessons unfold in the bonds we weave tight,
In the warmth of connection, we find our true light.

3. We Believed

When we were born in this world, we were a blank page
and we believed in everything we saw
Whatever was told to us by world for us we simply
believed and for us it became a law...

We wanted to keep everyone happy around us by
making the decisions of other's choices
More than working towards what we wanted we were
listening to other's voices...

We wanted to be a good child, sibling, wife, mother, and
best version of every relation
We lost ourselves in all of them and forgot that we are
losing our foundation....

It takes time to break the mould where we had been
living for so many decades
We forget we need to fight for our dreams and no one
comes to aides...

Once you decide and take a step out of your comfort
zone, destiny paves the way
Look around and take a sigh of relief to see so many
unwanted people sway...

Each and everyone of us have come in this world with a
predestined future
Always the first step is hardest, but the road to a happy
place is much smoother.

Close your eyes, dream and focus, see where and what
we want in our life...
You can still have a great future, no matter you are a
mother or the wife...

Emergence demands courage, a spark igniting from
within,
With wings of dawn, we rise anew, shedding yesterday's
skin.

For in the echoes of our heart, the whispers loud and
clear,
There's power in reclaiming self, in casting off the fear.

So stand tall in the light of your own desires, arms open
wide,
Embrace the beauty of your truth; let no one else decide.

4. Woman

To all the beautiful mornings with rays of hope and sun
shining through the cloud
So many times it weirdly feels lonely even when we are
in middle of crowd.

We do everything every day, repeatedly, and life
becomes a mechanical routine
We do not realize our human heart and mind also need a
regular clean.

Sometimes we are so habitual of unconsciously
becoming just a giver
We always look for someone to hold on to and turn into
their prisoner.

Whether it is work or home, we look for others'
acceptance and forget that we are valuable
When we believe ourselves as important to take
decisions, people mark us as trouble.

In the field of work, society thinks women cannot take
pressure and will crumble
Whereas a woman learns to be more patient, loving,
supporting, and humble.

Every woman has nature's best gift of being a
multitasker and emotionally strong,
She commits herself fully in work, relations, friendships,
always stays true to them till long.

But in the silence of her struggle, the depth of her dream
is quiet yet profound,
With whispers of strength, she rises, her spirit unbound,
softly breaking the ground.

For beyond the labels and limits, her essence weaves a
tapestry bright,
In unity with herself, she embodies the dawn,
transforming shadows into light.

Word Woman already has a man joined till the existence
of this World,
With love and companionship, they can create an
everlasting dreamworld.

Let them dance in the symphony of life, hand in hand
with grace,

Together they forge a path where every soul can find
their place.

5. Love

What is love if not a canvas, painted with every hue,
With strokes of joy and shades of sorrow, each breath a
story new?
In every gentle touch and shared glance, a universe
unfolds,
A testament to the beauty found in the tales that love
holds.

When distance stretches, and time may strain, it's
patience that will shine,
Through every doubt and every pain, it's trust that will
define.
For love's embrace is never weak, but a fortress standing
tall,
A bond that weathers every storm, forever, through it all.

In the twilight of our days, when memories softly gleam,

It's love that lingers in our hearts, the sweetest of all

dreams.

So what is love, if not the journey, hand in hand we take,

A symphony of souls combined, with every step we make?

6. Why didn't it happen

I gave my all and accepted everything and everyone with
whole heart and thought that we were on same page
I dreamt it was real for both of us and will last the same
always till we age...

Never could see beyond my love for you that you were
different and clear about what you meant with love and
relationship
I always took it as acceptance that what we started
together years back was unspoken and understood but
somewhere you took a slip...

I never changed my nature for any side of relations and
gave my all when it came to acceptance and opening our
home with all hearts
In this journey slowly realized that you had chosen your
side and divided relations in parts...

All this time I thought that we were dreaming and
working for both of us

I never bothered what you decided was right or wrong
and didn't make fuss...

Years passed and still wondering when and where I lost
that friend and lover of mine
Whenever we had problems, I was optimistic of letting it
pass and then we would be fine...

I was a cuddle lover and always expressive of my love
But never could find the spot where your feelings
shove...

With growing years and day to challenges, we were
supposed to be each other's support
Somewhere and somehow there came a distance where
we together could not deport...

I started talking more and more asking questions to
myself to find a solution
You made a choice and decided silence and distance was
your contribution...

I still being an optimistic, dream of a day where we will
sit again just as old times holding hands
We shall start it all together again and allow our love and
feeling to each other expand...

Being positive and coming out of problems has always
been a strength
No matter what and how problems come and whatever is
the time length....

We will win together as we were destined to meet and
stay
Whichever direction life takes us we will not sway...

Yet in the shadows of doubt, I cling to hope's bright
spark,
For love can rise anew, rekindling the flame from the
dark.

If only the echoes of silence could carry your name,
With every heartbeat whispering, I long to feel the same.

Let's weave through the silence and mend what we've
frayed,
Trusting the bond that once flourished, though now it's
decayed.

I'll wait for that moment when understanding ignites,
And together we'll journey, reclaiming old heights.

7. Express with gratitude and see things change

A human body is made up of so many different organs to
keep us alive
Same ways our emotions are related to every organ to
help us strive
Being Expressive is the best way to balance our mind,
body and relationship
It's possible for anyone to disagree to our thoughts
without affecting companionship
Sometimes a silence plays a positive role to keep
arguments away
Same silence while seeking resolution can result in
breaking away
It's very common to see people keeping to themselves at
work to avoid being called people pleaser
A place of no bonding and not standing for each other
shows the reality of organisation being a failure
A woman and a man can really make an excellent team,
But where a Woman is another woman's supporter,
that's the real place to be seen

The salary packages among colleagues should not be a
base of friendship or keeping a gap
The excellence and understanding of all team members
in their respective field is the result of their real growth
map
Sometimes it's important to be honest and be ready
always to face the challenge
For in vulnerability lies strength, and in truth, fighting
together Winning is the only chance..
Embrace the differences that flicker in our sights,
Collaboration births innovation, and unity ignites.
Let's weave our stories together, a tapestry of dreams,
In this shared endeavor, we can conquer the extremes.
So let's break the barriers, let the laughter unfurl,
For in every connection, we can uplift the world.
Hand in hand, we rise, through shadows and light,
In the heart of our efforts, we'll find the true might.
With compassion as our compass, and courage as our
guide,
Together, we'll navigate the changing tide.
In the symphony of voices, let harmony reign,
For when we unite, there is so much to gain.

8. ए काश वो दिन वापिस आ पाते

उन पुराने दिनों की यादें आज भी नींद में भी मुस्कुराहट चेहरे पे ले
आती हैं
पता नहीं क्या कशिश है उनमें, आज भी दिल में कसक दे जाती हैं

जब छोटे थे तो बस यही जुनून था कि बड़े होके दुनिया कदमों में रखा
करेंगे
कोई कभी भी कुछ भी समझाए बस पता था कि अपने ही मन की
सुना करेंगे

जो बचपन के थे यार दोस्त कभी उनके बारे में कोई खबर ही नहीं रही
ना जाने कितना सोचते दे पर फिर मन की बातें तब भी कही ही नहीं

बड़े पर्दे पे दिखते थे जो तो हीरो प्यार में मार देते दे या मारे जाते
बस बचपन में हमें तो यूँ लगता था , काश हम भी वैसे ही कुछ पल जी
पाते

समय बदला , बड़े हुए और ज़िंदगी में मोहब्बत भी मिली है हमको
असलियत में दोरती पहले चाहिए प्यार जैसे अनमोल रिश्ते निभाने
को

ज़िंदगी के सफ़र में आते बवण्डर ने कभी कभी तो ज़मीन भी हिलायी
थी
अपने दिल को समझाया और तैर के जीतने की क़सम ख़ुद से खायी
थी

ज़िंदगी के मीठे मीठे पल नींद में भी मुस्कुराहट दे जाते हैं
उन्हीं लम्हों को आँखों में संजोए हम बढ़े जाते हैं

छोटी सी कुटिया है मेरी जिसमे प्यार और नन्हे नन्हे सपने बसते हैं
प्यार की छाँव और हंसी के ठहाके से भरे पल बसते हैं

9. Love

Love is the gentle embrace that warms you on cold,
lonely nights
Love is the quiet moments when laughter dances in the
air like fireflies
Love is the rhythm of two hearts beating in sync, a
melody without a score
Love is the pulse that quickens in a crowded room, a
secret only you two know
Love is the threads that weave through life's fabric,
stitching memories with care
Love is the light that guides you home, even when the
path is unclear
Love is the adventure taken together, where every step is
a story untold
Love is the patience to listen, waiting for silence to break
into shared dreams
Love is the garden you cultivate, where trust blooms and
fears are laid to rest
Love is that quilt of imperfections, stitched with
laughter, tears, and grace.

10. वो लोग कौन हैं

रिश्ते और दोस्ती नाप के तोलने के लिए नहीं, महसूस करते हुए
निभाने के लिए होते हैं
कभी कभी इनको साथ लेके चलते हुए कभी हम सही तुम ग़लत, तो
कभी तुम सही और हम ग़लत होते हैं
रिश्ते में तुम्हारे ख़ून से जुड़े तुम्हें ज़्यादा प्यारे और मेरे ख़ून से जुड़े
तुम्हें ना गवारे नहीं हो सकते हैं
तुम्हारों ने तुम्हें प्यार और दुलार दिया, तो सब पहले और मेरे प्यारों की
तरफ़ हम नज़र कम नहीं कर सकते हैं

हर सपना तुम्हारा संजोने के लिए और तुम्हारा किया हर काम हमें सर
आँखों पे रखने के लिए क्यों होना ज़रूरी है
मेरी भी छोटी सी ही ज़िंदगी है, मेरे देखे और सोचे हुए ख़्वाब मुझे भी
हर साँस से ज़्यादा ज़रूरी है
एक छोटा सा घोंसला तिनका तिनका जोड़ के बनाया था, बड़ी मेहनत
और प्यार से
उसी घोंसले में तेरे मेरे ख़्वाबों, ख़्यालों और मंज़िलों के ना जाने हुए
हिस्से कब से

आज भी अनदेखी सी एक लकीर है जो एक दीवार सी बन के खड़ी है
हमारी मंज़िल के रास्ते पर

चाहे अगर तो हाथों में हाथ दे के गिरा दे और फेंक दे उसे दूर कहीं खाई पर

जब कभी वादा किया था साथ निभाने का एक दूसरे के साथ, तब कोई शर्त तो नहीं रखी थी हमने

फिर कब से दूसरे लोगों ने हमें ही अलग कर दिया हमारे ही बीच में

भूल ना जाना उन लम्हों को, जब नज़रें हमारी मिलती थीं चुपके से,
हर हंसी में छिपी थी कितनी बातें, हर आंसू की आवाज़ में गहराई थी,

रिश्तों की बुनाई में जो धागे हैं, उन्हें थामे रखना, यहीं है असली जीत,

चलो इसे फिर से जोड़ें, फिर से बनाएं वो घोंसला, जिसमें पलें हमारे ख्वाबों की रेल।

11. Where is God

If you close your eyes and sit on the floor, just feel the
ground underneath
Lift your head a little bit, back straight and empty your
mind and then slowly breathe
You will realize there is a power which you see like a
fastening light
The body leaves all the tension all of a sudden, and you
feel there is nothing to fight
The light you see transcends you to another world where
it's only you who matters
You see the white clouds and above that the sky which
really is pure and blue
You won't even realize that all this world exists only
within you but we never looked
Our body and mind demanded the peace and time away
from the chaos and the crowd
Our center of mind or between the brows is a place for
the creator, destroyer, and nurturer
He is always with us, or rather within us, only we need
to accept and be a little observer

We have been given the power to decide or to choose
between good or evil
We only become greedy day by day and just cross the
line and become devil

But within the silence, whispers echo clear, urging us to
reclaim the light,
To tread softly on this journey, where shadows dance,
but hope takes flight.
The path may twist and turn, burdened with choice, yet
wisdom chimes from within,
In the gentle embrace of stillness, let the truth stir and
begin.

Seek not just the outer brightness, but the glow that
flickers in your soul,
For when we delve into our depths, we rediscover
balance, we become whole.
Each choice a brushstroke on the canvas of life, each
breath a sacred song,
In the tapestry of existence, it is love that weaves us,
where we all belong.

12. Smile

Word SMILE has "So Many Important Lessons Earned "
hidden in itself
It has the power to face every day head on and also
cleaning ourself
A problem can take you the edge of a cliff and tempt you
to give up and fall down
If we change our perception towards the problem fight it
giggling and wear the Winning Crown
Sometimes Smile is the weapon which can decieve our
enemies and make them confused to what they aimed at
us
If we get affected and start showing it publicly then they
achieved what they wanted to achieve by breaking us
Whenever we feel that we can't carry it anymore, just
give yourself a last chance and try artificially to smile
more
The fake smile also has a power to free our mind and
body from the stress and anger
We will not ever realise when did we cross the thin line
of giving up and took ourselves away from danger

Our reflection in the mirror is where and how we want
to see ourselves
By wearing our smile constantly we keep pushing
ourself

13. मेरा जीवन मेरा संघर्ष

मैं भी कभी एक नन्ही सी परी थी,
मेरे भी आँखों में कई हंसीं सपने बसते थे।
जिस घर में हंसते माता पिता के साथ,
पास और दूर वाले सभी अपने थे।
माता पिता की हंसी भाई के गुज़ारने के सदमे ने छीन ली,
उस धक्के से उन्हें सँभालते हुए मैंने जीवन की सीख ली।

बड़े नाज़ों से पुचकारा था मैंने उन,
और मुश्किल से सम्भाला था उनको।
अनजाने में ही तू बहुत दूर कर गया था उन दोनों को,
वक्त के थपेड़ों ने सताया सदा उनको,
फिर भी जितना कोशिश हुआ सम्भाला उनको।

जब माँ का दर्द देखा ना गया,
पिता को समझाया मैंने,
माँ बनके डाँटा भी और उन्हें घर भिजवाया मैंने।
सदा यही आस थी कि दोनों सदा साथ साथ रहें,
जहां भी रहें, जैसे भी रहें, बाद वो आबाद रहें।

धीरे धीरे माँ ने भी लड़ाई छोड़ डाली,

एक दिन उन्होंने भी आख़िरी साँस ले डाली।
पिता जी को फिर भी न टूटने दिया मैंने,
जब भी मौक़ा मिला पास अपने बुलाया मैंने।

मैं पिता का सहारा और वो मेरी क़िस्मत थे,
कुछ कहते नहीं थे फिर हम सब समझते थे।
आख़िरी सफ़र पे निकल पड़े पिता जी भी एक दिन,
खबर सुनते ही अंदर तक टूट गई हिम्मत उस दिन।

सहेज के रखा मैंने उनके दिये आशीर्वाद को,
देखा करती थी आती थी याद उनकी जब भी।
अपने बच्चों को भी दर्द की भनक ना लगने दी,
हर मुस्कान में छुपा दिया मैंने उनका मान,
उनके दीए सपनों को मैंने सदा रखा सज़ा।

तुम तीनों मेरे आँखों के तारे और ज़िंदगी की कमायी हो,
मेरे पूरे जीवन करम के खेतों की तुम तीनों सिंचाई हो।
अपने पापा को मेरी तरफ़ से बाद इतना कह देना,
मैं सामने भले ना दिखूँ फिर भी तुम अच्छे से चलते रहना।

मेरा हाथ पकड़ कर नये रास्ते पे चलना सिखाया था तुमने,
अपने अंदर के दर्द को भूल कर भी कोशिश से हंसाया तुमने।
तुम सदा ख़ामोश रहते थे और मैं सदा कहती ही रही,
हर रिश्ते को निभाते हुए नदी की तरह बहती ही रही।

भगवान से मेरी बच्चों से हमेशा सदा एक ही शिक़ायत रही,
मेरे सुखों के लिए हमेशा उसकी आँख सदा मूँदी क्यों रही।

ना माँगा था चाँदी, सोना या आसमान मैंने,
बस एक छोटा सा अपना कोना चाहा था मैंने।

मुझे पता है बहुत सारे सवाल होंगे तुम सबके के मन में,
पता है ना तुम्हें कितने दर्द समेटे थे मन के साथ तन में।
मेरे सारे अधूरे काम और सपनों को तुम मिल के पूरा करना,
मेरे देने हुए भविष्य को और परिवार को तुम समेटे रखना।

ये ना समझना की मैंने तुम सब को अकेला छोड़ दिया सदा के लिए,
अब तो ऊपर वाले ने जादू की छड़ी भी दे दी हाथों में भले के लिए।
उस जहाँ से भी तुम्हारा ख़्याल रखती रहूँगी मैं बिना दिखे हुए भी,
जब भी सपना कोई पूरा हो तो समझ लेना की छड़ी घूमी भी।

कोशिशों का दीप जलाना, राहों में न डरना,
जो भी छाया गहरा हो, तुम उसे चुनौती देना।
दिल में प्यार बसा रखना, हिम्मत को कभी ना खोना,
याद रखोगी तुम, मेरी लोरियाँ गूंजती रहेंगी, हर सुकून में तुम्हारा नाम
होगा, हर खुशी में मेरा चेहरा आँखों में संजो के रात को सोना

14. Dream n Believe

There is a world where clouds meet us on the road and
makes it magical
There is peace , nature and greenery in abundance and
lifestyle is ethical
Days can go being busy at work but evenings for only all
of us together
Where the arguments, anger and ego stays out of the
door and doesn't bother
Transition is only challenging but not difficult to achieve
We always get bothered and get hassled and grieve
What can be difficult looking might change our all
perceptions
We might just gel and blend in everything smoothly and
can be exceptions
Let's all take that very step with a belief and promise to
be together always till our breaths last
It will be a lovely life full of love and laughter and time
will go fast

15. Be Kind

In a world that's wide and full of light,
We grow like trees in morning bright.
With roots of love, deep in the ground,
And wings of dreams that lift us sound.
Be kind, my child, with every word,
A gentle voice is always heard.
Treat others as you'd like to be—
With open heart and honesty.
Respect is more than being nice,
It's showing care, not thinking twice.
It's helping hands and listening ears,
And standing strong through others' tears.
Share your laughter, share your toys,
Include all girls and all the boys.
What you give will come to stay,
In brighter hearts along the way.
Forgive with grace, don't hold on tight
To angry thoughts or wrongs or spite.
For peace will grow where grudges cease,
And broken bonds will mend in peace.

Your family, friends, and neighbors too,
Are precious gifts entrusted to you.
So cherish them, be brave and true—
And they'll give love right back to you.
Remember this: the world begins
With kindness, courage, and some wins.
But most of all, the love you give—
Will shape the life you choose to live

16. A Life of Peace and Love

In quiet moments, hearts unfold,
Far more precious than coins or gold.
A smile, a touch, a kind reply—
These light the soul, like stars the sky.
No rush, no race, just steady grace,
With love to fill each time and place.
A gentle word, a helping hand,
Can build a world where all hearts stand.
So may we walk with open eyes,
Beneath the calm of endless skies—
Where peace and love, in softest light,
Turn every day from dark to bright
The days awaited full of love and laughter
All the struggles we had wouldn't matter
Fighting together makes us stronger and ready for
another flight
No matter how long or delayed the results be, we will
catch the Sunlight

17. Trust the Divinity

Watches over us gently, a guardian through each sigh.
In moments of doubt when shadows creep near,
Reach out in silence, draw strength from the sphere.
For the heart knows the rhythm, the pulse of the divine,
In whispered prayers, our spirits entwine.

So let hope be a beacon, a light in the night,
Guiding us onward, igniting our fight.
Even in sorrow, when darkness seems vast,
Remember the lessons, the shadows are cast.

Embrace every challenge, each fear that we face,
For every setback is part of a grace.
Trust in the journey, the purpose behind,
For within each struggle, true treasures we find.

And if doubts should arise, like clouds in the sky,
Know that every storm passes, they too must comply.
For the soul's quiet courage, when nourished with care,
Can rise like a phoenix, meet life with a flare.

18. घोंसला प्यारा

आज अपने बच्चों की उड़ने की बारी आयी है
सपने उनके भी पूरे होंगे मैंने भी क़सम खायी है
बस अपनी छांव में एक-एक बूँद ख़ुशी सिंचती जाओंगी
उनकी राहों में अंगारों की बजाए फूल बिछाती जाओंगी

उड़ान के लिए छोड़ दूंगी वो सुरक्षित घोंसला प्यारा
उनके अंदर की चिड़िया को दे दूंगी उड़ने का सहारा
जब भी ठोकर लगे, याद दिलाना मेरा प्यार भरा समर्पण
हर गिरने पर उठ खड़े होना, यही है असली जीवन का रत्न

उन्हें भी चाहिए हिम्मत, जैसे माँ बाबा ने मुझे सिखाया था
हर सफर की कठिनाई में मैंने अपना सब कुछ पाया था
उनकी आँखों में देखूंगी मैं एक नया आसमान चमकता
और गर्व से कहूंगी, मेरे बच्चों, तुमने सपनों को खोला, नया सफर
लिखा

19. Friends

Friends are the extended family whose calls and presence
brighten our evenings after a tiring day
They can be pushy, irritating but mostly end up making
feel us like child who wants to play

It can be simple gup shop over Chai or evening filled
with music, dance with the drinks
The closer you get to each other the good time we spend
laughing ,enjoying goes in eye-blinks

It starts with the focus on everyone trying to have good
time to forget their own battle
The bond we develop over the time by being their with
each other ,the struggles seem to settle

The achievements of friends feel like we won a
competition and got a prize
Sometimes we can't even sense but they cheer you up
and plan a surprise

We might be living around each other for long but some
day move and change places
Still our routine carries on through out but always
searching for those smiling faces

So whenever you make a friend just make sure you hold
them close to heart
Their presence and support in our life can change a weak
person into a brave heart

They are not related to us by blood but what we
exchange is precious and true
In deepest losses when we are drowning they hold your
hand and carry you

The crazy songs sung on high volume come straight
from heart with the silly dances moves
The special days becomes extra special and the quality of
life, thoughts and ideas definitely improves

Their presence can light up dull face and their absence
can leave a vacuum
We know we are to be their forever and say bye with the
promise to see each other soon

So be greedy to hold on to the moments, cherish them
who walks beside

They never leave us alone ,flinch and never ever hide
The greatest gift we give ourselves is simply our
FRIENDS

20. Inner Child

To never let our inner child grow up should be our
mission,
This will always help everyone to go through life's
transition.
If we just assess life's challenges with that child's point
of view,
That child will just face it — with wonder shining
through.
Where adults see failure, the child sees a game,
Each fall just a lesson, never a shame.
With eyes full of questions, not judgments or fear,
The child seeks adventure in all that is near.
They dance through the rain, not worrying why,
They laugh at the storm, and paint on the sky.
Their hearts remain open, unburdened, unbound,
Hearing the music in the softest of sound.
So let's hold that child, don't lock them away,
Let them guide our steps, come what may.
For in their small hands lies infinite grace,
A light that can brighten the darkest place.

So let's make this promise, both steady and wild—
To live with the wonder and heart of a child

21. Treasure of Life is Health

A good Health is an inexpensive gift we should all give
ourselves
It fills our life with all joy and doesn't need to be
purchased from shelves
It is the core of our life which has been gifted to us on
which we stand
We do so much for fun same way to stay healthy also
needs to be planned

As they say we become and think what we eat and how
we move
Whatever we put in our stomach the choices we make
will decide if our life can improve
Eating the freshly cooked food, seasonal fresh veggies
and fruits can make us healthy and lean too
Eating in balance and with discipline for sleep, and
exercise all together help us renew

We may earn enormously and live lavishly but shouldn't
ignore being happy and healthy
It's something we must cherish and makes us genuinely
wealthy

With it, we can spend good time with our family and
friends as we please
Being there for our loved one's without any fears but to
live life to the fullest with grace and ease

So let's make our health a top priority
And work to keep it in good quality
For when we are healthy, we can achieve
Anything we dream, and truly believe.

www.ingramcontent.com/pod-product-compliance
Lightning Source LLC
LaVergne TN
LVHW050948200726
843508LV00011B/2471